In Search of the Spirit

The Living National Treasures of Japan

by Sheila Hamanaka and Ayano Ohmi

illustrations by Sheila Hamanaka • *calligraphy by* Ayano Ohmi

Morrow Junior Books • New York

Japan forms a crescent 1,860 miles long. Until about twelve thousand years ago the mountainous land was the coast of the continent of Asia, stretching from what is now Siberia to Korea. But with the end of the Ice Age the polar ice to the north of Japan melted and the oceans rose, isolating the people who lived on that coast. Now four main islands—Honshu, Shikoku, Kyushu, and Hokkaido—and over four thousand others make up a country about the size of California.

Hot and cold ocean currents circle the islands, and seasonal typhoons throw down torrents of wind and water. Huge volcanic mountain ranges arch their backs and shudder with earthquakes. This environment forged a hardworking people filled with a deep respect for and love of nature. And nature is the inspiration for the Living National Treasures of Japan.

CONTENTS

WHO ARE THE LIVING NATIONAL TREASURES?

In a small town a sword maker hammers out a flawless weapon over a glowing fire. Miles away, an actor in breathtaking silk robes dons a mask and turns into a demon. And in the shadow of a mountain, knife in hand, a man splits a length of bamboo into wisps and weaves an intricate basket. These are scenes out of the sixteenth century, but they are still taking place in Japan today.

Isolated by the sea for centuries, the Japanese were inspired by the ancient civilizations of India, Korea, and especially China. By A.D. 600 many were crossing the treacherous seas and bringing back fabulous treasures—works of art, new ideas about religion, science, and law, and even the Chinese system of writing. These were the precious seeds of Japanese culture.

Three centuries later, Japan was a prosperous country famous for the quality of its design and craftsmanship. The ruling classes, and later, wealthy landowners, merchants, and the religious establishment, demanded the finest weapons, clothing, and works of art and craft. These unique creations were produced by families who passed on their sometimes secret skills from generation to generation.

During World War II, much of Japan was destroyed, including many of its ancient monuments and works of art. People felt a deep sense of loss. Machines were replacing hardworking artisans, and age-old traditions were disappearing. What could be done?

In the 1950s Japan decided to honor the elders who had devoted their lives to traditional crafts and performing arts. These individuals were given grants to practice their arts and to train apprentices. Today over one hundred men and women have been given the special title of Bearers of Important Intangible Cultural Assets. (The word *intangible* means something that cannot be touched but only sensed.) They are popularly called Living National Treasures.

All of these masters share a simple view: There is no substitute for hard work. Their own training is lifelong. Yet they also insist that even the most perfect technique will fail unless it springs from deep feeling. They themselves have listened closely and heard the souls of the old masters whispering to them from the past. Through their magnificent arts the Living National Treasures *are* passing on something intangible—the spirit of Japan's unique culture.

Note: In Japan, the family (or "last") name is written first, followed by the person's given name. We follow that practice in this book.

MORIGUCHI KAKO
YUZEN DYER

"I've always encouraged myself through my belief that hope is a great treasure in our lives. . . . I keep studying without stopping."

Moriguchi Kako (MOR-EE-GOO-CHEE KAH-KO) sits on the floor in front of a large low worktable in his studio. He has devoted his life to decorating kimonos, the traditional costumes worn by Japanese people for centuries. In order to create his beautiful designs on silk, Mr. Moriguchi uses a unique method of dyeing called yuzen (YOO-ZEN). He is famous for his fresh, bold treatment of traditional Japanese subjects, such as flowers, water, and trees. Each kimono he creates is one of a kind and is treasured as a family heirloom. But now he is worried. For him, the kimono is a way of life, and it may be passing away.

Yuzen dyeing was invented about three hundred years ago in the city of Kyoto (KYO-TOE). At that time Japan was strictly divided into social and political

Left, *a finished kimono is displayed;* middle, *an example of Mr. Moriguchi's own technique, called makinori;* right, *Moriguchi Kako paints his signature in Japanese calligraphy on every kimono. (Calligraphy is an elegant form of handwriting.)*

classes. At the top was the shogun, or military dictator, and his samurai warriors. Peasants and skilled workers were next. Merchants were looked down upon as the lowest class. Because clothing was one way to tell who was important and who was not, by law only the ruling class wore colorful, expensive kimonos made from imported Chinese silk brocades. But the townspeople and merchants were becoming more prosperous, and they wanted to be fashionable too. Since they weren't allowed to wear fancy brocades, artists invented new ways to decorate plainer silks for them. The most famous method was yuzen, based on an East Indian process called batik.

Mr. Moriguchi bases his designs on sketches from nature.

Mr. Moriguchi was born in 1909. He loved to paint, but at twelve he had to give up school and become an apprentice in a pharmacy. He was sad, but every day he put his drawings of goldfish and animals in the shop window.

When Mr. Moriguchi was fifteen, a famous painter and yuzen dyer named Nakagawa Kason saw his work and was very impressed. He invited the young man to his workshop. As Mr. Moriguchi watched the artists painting beautiful yuzen designs, he knew he had found his life's work. At that time young people in Japan were not encouraged to make their own choices in life. Nonetheless, Mr. Moriguchi defied his father and became one of Nakagawa's apprentices.

For three years Mr. Moriguchi only ran errands. He learned by watching.

Above, *Mr. Moriguchi's worktable*; below, *the artist as a boy*

When he was finally allowed to paint, Mr. Moriguchi had to practice and copy the designs day after day. He had only two days off every month.

When he was thirty years old, Mr. Moriguchi finally opened his own yuzen workshop. "I still work hard every day," he says. "In my pocket I carry pieces of paper on which the kimono shape is already drawn. Anytime an idea comes to my mind, I start to draw."

Mr. Moriguchi is proud that he can see what others miss at first: empty space! "The starting point of drawing and painting is to concentrate on the

Left, the use of space is an important idea in Japanese art.

notion of space. . . . When you draw tree branches, you should look at a branch and at the shape of the space that is around the branch. As you do, you will begin to appreciate the beauty of empty space."

Mr. Moriguchi is one of the few artists who still decorate kimonos the traditional way, completely by hand. He feels his most important task as a Living National Treasure is to preserve the technique of yuzen by nurturing young artists. He's taken on ten apprentices, including his son, Kunihiko. They all now work independently.

MORE ABOUT YUZEN

It takes up to eight weeks to complete a kimono. Working closely with an assistant, Moriguchi Kako follows these steps:

1. Pieces of white silk are stitched together into the shape of a kimono. Then the design is sketched on the kimono with a charcoal pencil.

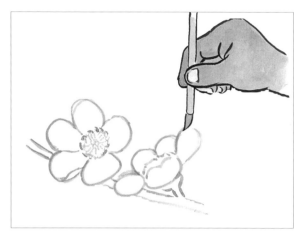

2. The charcoal sketch is painted over with a small brush dipped in blue ink made from an aobana (AH-OH-BAH-NA) flower. The kimono is displayed, so the artist can see if the design looks balanced.

3. Then the kimono is taken apart, and the pieces are stretched smooth on bamboo frames.

4. With a tsutsugami (TSOO-TSOO-GAH-ME), a tool something like a cake decorator, a dye-resistant paste is squeezed over the blue lines. This will help keep the colors from running together. Mr. Moriguchi always does this himself to give the line feeling.

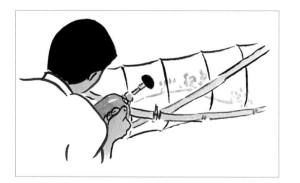

5. Then the fabric is sprayed with water. This removes the charcoal and the blue lines but leaves the paste lines.

6. The pieces are dried quickly over a charcoal fire.

8. The fabric is steamed to fix the dyes and restretched onto the bamboo frames.

9. All the painted areas are covered with a resist starch to protect them while color is applied to the background.

7. A soybean solution is applied to improve the colors and, like the paste lines, to keep them from running. Then dyes are painted onto the fabric.

11. These flakes are sprinkled onto the damp fabric. The flakes stick and resist the color that is brushed on, which results in a speckled look. This technique may be repeated several times at different stages.

12. The background color is brushed on. The fabric is dried and again steamed to fix the dyes.

10. Mr. Moriguchi has added a new twist to yuzen, called makinori (MAH-KEE-NO-REE). For this effect, crushed flakes of dye-resistant paste are separated by size.

14. The fabric is dried and basted together and given a final steaming to make sure all the pieces fall correctly. At long last, the pieces are sewn into a kimono.

13. The fabric is soaked and washed by hand to remove the paste. This may be repeated several times.

13

IIZUKA SHOKANSAI
BAMBOO WEAVER

"You should be aware of the seeds of feeling in your heart and take care of them. And try to express the feeling sincerely and honestly."

A small green mountain looks down on Iizuka Shokansai's (E-ZOO-KA SHOW-KAHN-SIGH) home. Fittingly, his garden is surrounded with tall graceful bamboo trees. For this is his specialty: bamboo baskets.

To Mr. Iizuka, weaving baskets is a fine art. He never makes the same piece twice. He loves bamboo and so does the rest of Asia. For over three thousand years, people have made homes, tools, baskets, and chopsticks out of bamboo. They even eat the tender shoots. There are more than twelve hundred different types of bamboo plants in the world, and half can be found in Japan.

Bamboo basket weaving found its way to Japan from China, India, and other Asian countries. Then the new popular craze for serving tea created an even greater

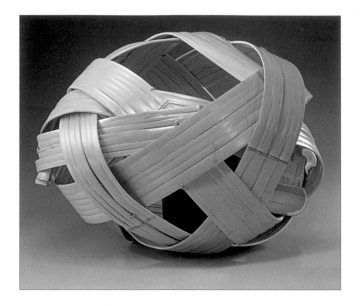

Iizuka Shokansai's creations are works of art; right, tools with splints of bamboo

demand for bamboo craftsmanship. The tea ceremony began as an artistic ritual and then became the rage among the Japanese nobility and the wealthy merchants who liked to copy them—and it required whisks and other utensils made of bamboo.

Japanese traditions sometimes seem as permanent as its mountains, and of these traditions, family obligation looms very large. A child is supposed to respect and obey the parent. In Japan, the task of carrying on the family business usually falls on the shoulders of the oldest son.

Iizuka Shokansai's father, like his father before him, was an influential bamboo weaver. But as the second son, Mr. Iizuka felt free to follow his own dreams. He attended the most famous art school in Japan and studied painting. However, when his older brother died in the 1940s, everything changed.

Mr. Iizuka now had to take care of all family matters, including maintaining the bamboo workshop. At thirty years of age, he knew that it was late to start learning his father's art, but there was no choice. He gave up spending time

with his friends and devoted all of his time and energy to bamboo. It was a very difficult decision.

Mr. Iizuka knew that the way of bamboo was a hard one. He knew that the first step—learning how to cut bamboo—was said to take ten years. In the traditional Japanese way of apprenticeship, there is no such thing as reading textbooks, writing papers, and getting a degree. Mr. Iizuka learned by watching and trying to imitate his father, who was very strict. Mr. Iizuka's progress was slow. He often felt frustrated and disappointed, but he never gave up.

And in the end, as he will tell you, it takes more than years of training to make great art. For Mr. Iizuka, the secret lies in the heart. "The more excited you feel while creating, the more your work can move the viewer's feelings. Since vases and boxes are things for use, people tend to judge them by how useful they are. Therefore it is especially difficult and challenging for the artist to go beyond this point of view and create powerful and impressive works of art out of everyday things. For this to be possible, you must always nurture your heart."

More about Bamboo Weaving

Every November Iizuka Shokansai goes to the bamboo fair in Kyoto. The very first step is choosing the right bamboo. The green bamboo is bleached and dried in the sun for two to three months. Mr. Iizuka is famous for his tabaneami (TAH–BAH–NAY–AH–ME) technique, in which a basket is made from a single length of bamboo. This process may take three months or more from start to finish. These are the basic steps:

1. Mr. Iizuka first draws a rough sketch. Next comes a detailed drawing that shows all the patterns he will weave into the basket. Mr. Iizuka figures out how many splints he will need from one length of bamboo, and their exact size.

2. It takes about a month just to prepare the bamboo. Mr. Iizuka begins by polishing a length of bamboo.

3. Using a sharp knife, he smoothes down the joints of the bamboo.

4. The bamboo is split in half.

5. and 6. Using a short, very sharp blade, Mr. Iizuka cuts the bamboo into finer and finer strips. He has to measure and cut very precisely.

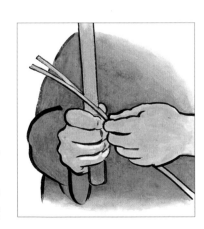

7. Each splint is drawn under a sharp blade to shave it down to exactly the right size.

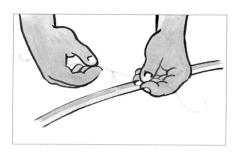

8. The splints are tied into bundles.

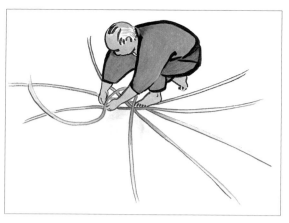

9. Using his foot to hold everything together, Mr. Iizuka begins weaving the bundles.

10. A bowl of water is always nearby to keep the bamboo wet.

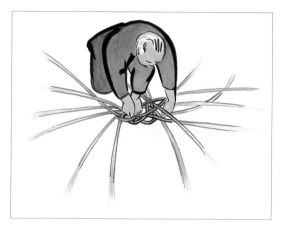

11. The bamboo is wet to keep it flexible. The splints may be over three yards long and can easily snap. One broken splint ruins the whole basket.

12. and 13. As he works upward, Mr. Iizuka follows his original drawing as closely as possible.

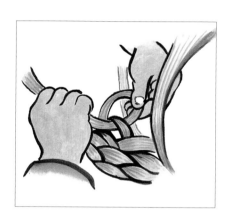

14. and 15. By weaving the bamboo in bundles or separately, splint by splint, he is able to create many different patterns.

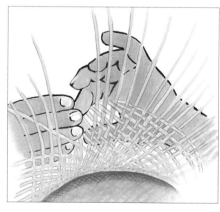

16. and 17. If the pattern calls for very fine weaving, the tiny splints are cut with the aid of a magnifying glass.

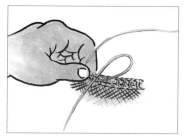

18. The finest strands may be added as a finishing touch.

YOSHIDA MINOSUKE
BUNRAKU PUPPET MASTER

"I'm not interested in copying the way the former masters interpreted the stories. I study what our masters did or are doing now, and I digest it, adding my own interpretation to the movement. I like something new, meeting a challenge."

It's rehearsal time at the Osaka Bunraku (BOON-RAH-KOO) Theater. The halls backstage bustle with activity as men dressed all in black carry trunks and puppets. In a dressing room shared by several performers a man kneels, fitting a costume onto a puppet. It is Yoshida Minosuke (YO-SHE-DA ME-NO-SKEH), famous master puppeteer.

Mr. Yoshida's father, also a puppeteer, didn't want his son to follow in his footsteps. He knew that the training was painful and that it was hard to get roles. But even as a tiny child Mr. Yoshida was caught in the spell of the Bunraku puppets. So, when he was only six years old, he left his family to become an apprentice to a puppeteer named Yoshida Bungoro.

*The chanter
and shamisen
player perform;
right, Yoshida
Minosuke fits
a costume onto
a puppet frame.*

The art of Bunraku was born over four centuries ago in Osaka, the commercial capital of Japan. There, the growing class of wealthy townspeople demanded entertainment. The puppeteers put on irresistible shows that combined storytelling and music. In a Bunraku performance, a lively chanter speaks all the roles played by the puppets and often bursts into song. He sits next to a musician who plays a shamisen, a three-stringed instrument. Other musicians may perform onstage, and offstage, too. Altogether there are about eighty-five singers, musicians, and puppeteers in the troupe.

For hundreds of years the training for Bunraku puppeteers has been the same. It takes three people—by tradition, all men—to operate one puppet. A master like Mr. Yoshida, who works only the puppet's head and right hand, first must spend ten years working the puppet's legs and fifteen more years working its left hand. In Bunraku, no one is ever an overnight success!

Handling a Bunraku puppet is hard work. The puppets weigh anywhere

Rehearsals for Hirakana Seisui Ki. *This play, first performed in 1739, dramatizes a historic battle between two warring clans. Mr. Yoshida, famous for playing women, is the head puppeteer for the lead character, Ofude, left.*

from ten to fifty pounds, and some are almost five feet tall. Mr. Yoshida began to perform when he was twelve or thirteen years old. "My spine is bent. I was trained how to manipulate the puppet's legs when my body was growing. I squeezed myself into a limited space between two puppeteers for a long time, day after day, either practicing or performing, and I just couldn't grow straight after that. My left hand is bigger than my right hand, because I hold the puppet's head with my left hand."

In Japan it is considered important to work well in groups. Nowhere is this more true than in Bunraku, where it takes three people to operate one puppet in time with the other puppeteers. It took Mr. Yoshida a long time to learn

In these rehearsal scenes, puppets waiting to perform, at left, become oarsmen in the play, right. On the opposite page, a character loyal to one of the warring clans is set upon by the oarsmen of the other!

how to breathe while manipulating a puppet, and how to eliminate any excess movements on stage.

Bunraku stories are often tragedies about war or unhappy lovers, as they are in Noh theater. These classic plays were written for, and watched by, adults. Mr. Yoshida's company also puts on special plays for children.

Mr. Yoshida finds that the audience is always surprised at how human the puppets appear, so much so that they often forget they are at a puppet performance. He always feels an emotional energy flowing between the stage and the audience. This is the source of the magic that captivated him as a child.

"This energy exchange, this wave of feelings gets extremely hot. This moment is the highest peak of creation. In order to create this moment, and to pull that wave of emotion out of the audience, I devote my time to practicing. To this process there is no end."

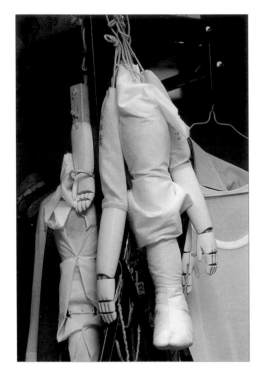

More about Bunraku

A lot goes on behind the scenes at the Osaka Bunraku Theater. Artists and craftspeople work tirelessly, as they have done for hundreds of years, to create and maintain the exquisite puppets and costumes. Puppeteers like Yoshida Minosuke do a lot more than just perform—they literally shape the characters of their puppets.

1. Puppet heads, hands, arms, and legs are carved by a master sculptor out of Japanese cypress. The heads are hollow and fitted with eyes. On some puppets, the eyes, mouths, and eyebrows can move, controlled by hidden strings.

2. Puppeteers assemble the bodies of their own puppets.

3. Shoulder boards are carved from wood. Shoulder pads, shaped to fit the age, sex, and personality of the character, are made from loofah sponges. Arms and legs are attached with ropes to the shoulder board.

4. A bamboo hoop forms the hips. Female puppets have no legs, since they are always dressed in skirts.

5. A wig master prepares the puppets' wigs. The wigs are made from human or yak hair. Wig masters know how to fashion over a hundred different hairstyles.

6. Handmade costumes are sewn onto the puppets by the puppeteers.

7. Backstage, lifelike puppets wait to perform.

8. As seen in this rehearsal, major characters are controlled by three puppeteers. At a performance, everyone wears a black hood except the master puppeteer.

9. Mr. Yoshida is most famous for bringing heroines to life.

10. This exciting rehearsal is alive with the magic of Bunraku.

27

日本刀

SUMITANI MASAMINE
SWORD MAKER

"I always try to do what I like."

The room is dark. The only light comes from a high tiny window. In one corner there are baskets full of coal, and hanging on the wall, there are tools that look like giant pliers. The brick floor has been swept clean of ashes. This is the workshop of one of Japan's greatest living sword makers, Sumitani Masamine (SOO-ME-tah-nee MAH-SAH-ME-NEH). Mr. Sumitani stands modestly to the side, looking as if he were made partly of smoke and ashes himself, with a wisp of a body and graying hair.

The imperial sword of Japan, by legend, was pulled by a god from the tail of an eight-headed dragon. It was a sacred object. In ancient Japan only the ruling class and their samurai were allowed to carry swords, and they could legally cut down any commoner who offended them. Japanese swords, folded and pounded over and

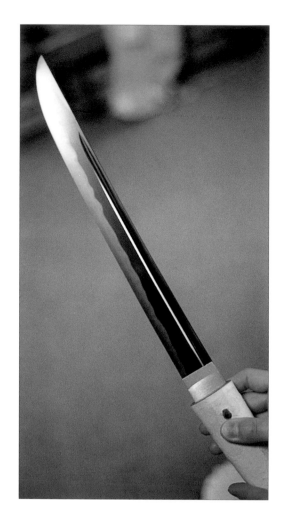

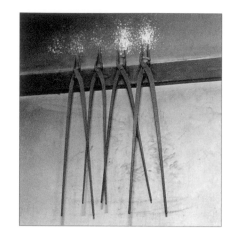

Left, *on this small sword can be seen the distinctive hamon (HA-MONE), or wave pattern;* middle and right, *tongs and baskets of coal in Sumitani Masamine's workshop.*

over again into more than a million layers, are said to be the strongest in the world. They are also said to carry the spirit of their makers.

As a young man, Mr. Sumitani was a rebel. His parents were in the soy sauce business, and they expected their son to carry on the family tradition. But then Mr. Sumitani saw a sign that changed his life—it read Japanese Sword Forging Institute. Mysteriously, the sign seemed to call to him. Japan was in the midst of World War II, but Mr. Sumitani's poor health had kept him out of the army. He felt lost and worried about the outcome of the war. Impulsively, he decided to enter the institute. It was the beginning of his lifelong study of the traditional techniques of sword making.

His parents were upset. To them, sword making was just a hobby. Nevertheless, Mr. Sumitani began studying night and day.

"I often felt alone practicing sword making," he says, "especially when my friend, another apprentice, died from tuberculosis in 1943. I didn't have family support, and there were no sword masters in my family's past. I found it would be my destiny to work alone for my entire lifetime."

In 1943 Mr. Sumitani won his first award for sword making. But after Japan

Mr. Sumitani also makes knives, shown here in their elegant sheaths, or coverings.

lost World War II, all weapons were banned, including swords. Mr. Sumitani went back to the family business. Then, in 1953, it was decided that a sword was needed for a sacred Shinto religious rite held every twenty years at the ancient Ise Jingu (EE-SAY JEEN-GOO) shrine. To be selected for the competition became the highest honor among the sword masters. In the following year, Mr. Sumitani was certified by the government as a master sword maker, and in 1973 one of his swords was chosen for the Ise Jingu rite.

Even now, by law, sword makers are allowed to produce only two swords per month. The maker has to be certified by the government. A five-year apprenticeship under a certified master is a requirement.

When Mr. Sumitani sees the flawless work of the old masters, he stands straighter because he knows he is in the presence of great works of art. He feels the spirits of the master sword makers speaking to him through the centuries.

MORE ABOUT SWORD MAKING

In the West, most swords are formed from one type of steel, which is a mixture of iron and carbon. In Japan, however, swords are formed from a special combination of three kinds of steel that contain varying amounts of carbon. The sword maker starts with almost twenty pounds of metal, but in the end, after all the impurities and carbon have been beaten out, the blade weighs just over two pounds. The sword is composed of two layers: an inner core of softer steel and an outer layer of harder steel. The blade of a long sword is about 3 1/2 feet long.

1. A graceful sword starts out as a hunk of iron ore.

2. Carbon is added, and the metal is forged, or heated and beaten, into wafers of steel called jigane (JEE-GAH-NEH).

3. The jigane is doused with muddy water mixed with clay. Straw ash is applied, and it is heated over handmade pine charcoal. The water and ash keep the steel surface from getting too hot, which would weaken the blade.

4. After thirty minutes, the metal is taken out of the fire. It is beaten first with a small hammer, then with a large sledgehammer. Steps 3 and 4 are repeated six or seven times.

5. A cut is made in the middle of the metal with a chisel.

6. The hot metal is then folded in half and pounded again. This folding and pounding process is repeated fifteen to twenty times for the outer skin, and five to eight times for the inner core.

7. The sword is pounded and folded over and over until it consists of over a million layers of steel! This, along with the special combination of steels, makes it the strongest sword in the world.

8. The outer layer is carefully wrapped around the inner core and the two layers are forged together. The sword is shaped with a scraping knife and metal files.

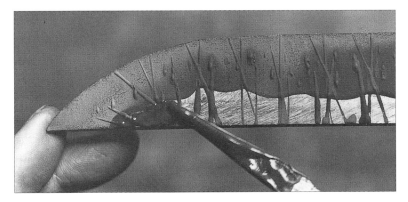

9. Then it is splashed with a special blend of straw ash and red mud. Exactly how the mud is splashed on is a top secret of every sword-making family. This step produces the unique signature pattern called hamon.

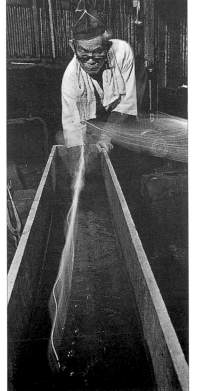

10. The blade is put back into the fire. Then it is plunged, red-hot, into water—for just two-tenths of a second! Then the sword is sharpened and polished on a whetstone.

33

KANZE TETSUNOJO
NOH ACTOR

"There is an exchange of feeling between my role with a mask and myself. . . . There is invisible energy moving between self, role, and audience."

On a wooden stage, an older man and a young boy face each other. Suddenly the man swings a long pike and the boy leaps into the air with perfect timing. They do it again—and again.

Kanze Tetsunojo (KON-ZEH TEH-TSOO-NO-JO), a famous actor, is training Rentaro, the fourteen-year-old son of another actor in his troupe. The boy's father watches intently. This is serious business. For this young boy, being on the stage means more than just having fun in a school play. This theater will become his life.

Noh, the elegant and mysterious drama of aristocratic Japan, has its roots in the rice fields. For hundreds of years villagers, priests, and performers—singers, dancers, musicians, magicians, and acrobats—acted out plays that

Left, *Kanze Tetsunojo performing in a play called* Hagoromo; right and opposite page, *some expressive Noh masks*

celebrated and prayed to the gods for a good rice crop and long life. The bored court nobles invited these performers in to entertain them.

By the fifteenth century Noh had changed completely from those earlier celebrations. It had taken on the qualities most prized by the nobility—beauty, elegance, and restraint.

Like poetry, and unlike most western drama, Noh often has no plot. The tales, traditionally written by the actors themselves, often deal with death. Noh developed in an era of feudal warfare, when thoughts about death were on people's minds. Life seemed to reflect the ideas of Buddhism, which held that life is suffering and that true life begins after death. So the stories are tragic tales about human fate and often tell of terrible battles between clans.

The main actor in Noh is called Shite (SHE-TEH). The Shite actor usually wears a mask and plays a wide range of roles, from ordinary people to gods, demons, ghosts, and even animals. Waki (WHA-KEE) is the character who asks questions as Shite wanders the stage and tells the story, seeking either revenge or peace.

Like a Japanese painting or a haiku poem, everything in a Noh play is simplified

Top right, *the unique wooden stage used in Noh, with its backdrop of a simple pine tree*

to the bare essentials. There are only a few actors. The special wooden stage has no scenery except for an ancient pine tree painted on the back wall. The spare, poetic language is sung and danced to music. Most of the time the actors move in slow motion. A simple gesture tells the audience that someone has taken a long journey, or is sobbing in pain. The actors sing and dance while a chorus of eight to ten men sings the narration. Musicians sit on stage behind the actors and play two or three drums and a flute.

Because of the slow and serious nature of Noh plays, they are often performed with short comedies called Kyogen (KYO-GEN). A full, formal program consists of five Noh plays and four Kyogen plays. It goes on all day, with a long lunch break.

Below, Mr. Kanze performing as a boy, and right, in the "mirror room," a special place where Noh actors put on their masks and transform themselves into their characters before going onstage. Far right, Mr. Kanze, in the white wig, and another actor are dressed as lions in a play called Shakkyo.

Mr. Kanze plays the Shite role, a tradition in his family since the fourteenth century.

When he was three years old, Mr. Kanze made his first appearance on stage. By five or six, if he walked through his role smoothly and soundlessly, without any mistakes, he got some sweets. Soon he started to perform as the child companion of an adult warrior or master. Often he had to sit still without moving for more than one hour. Now it is Mr. Kanze who trains very small children. And for Mr. Kanze, as for the other Living National Treasures, there are no textbooks about his art. When he teaches the movements of Noh, it is always person to person, master to student.

Traditionally, all the roles in Noh are played by men. Mr. Kanze often plays

the role of a woman. He dons a woman's robes and the mask of a woman's face, but sings with his natural man's voice. The effect is haunting.

The mask is the heart of a Noh performance. Actors treat masks with great respect and go through a special ritual when they put one on.

"Through the eyes of a mask you don't see much . . . also you can't breathe very well. . . . The first time I wore a mask onstage I felt pressed in. I was about nineteen years old. I felt totally alone in a pitch-dark world.

"I feel very special when I wear an old mask made in the eighteenth century, one that has been worn over one hundred times by our former masters. Can you imagine it? I feel their sweat on the masks. Through the mask all these powerful things cross over time and pass on to me."

MORE ABOUT NOH

Noh actors move in a very special way. Their walk is more like a ghostly glide. You can often "read" what's going on in a scene—including the weather—if you know the meaning of each of the gestures they make. Here are just a few gestures that Kanze Tetsunojo might use in a performance.

1. Mist fan: When an open fan is lowered until it parallels the floor, it suggests mist, waterfalls, or wind in the mountains.

2. Moon fan: The actor touches his left shoulder with an open fan and looks up and to his right, showing that there is a moon in the sky.

3. Pillow fan shows the actor taking a nap.

4. Inviting fan: When an actor raises the fan up and down, his character is calling someone or showing affection.

5. This is a gesture that usually indicates joy. The actor holds the fan to his chest and moves it to the right, then repeats the motion.

6. This gesture shows grief or weeping.

7. Here the fan represents a shield . . .

8. and here, a sword.

MATSUI KOSEI
POTTER

"Once you reach the highest level, you are free."

Dampness and hot weather envelop Kasama, a small town northwest of Tokyo, shutting out noise and hurry. Tall trees, bamboo and pine, hover over the Gessho-ji (GESH-SHOW-JEE) temple, and their scents are mixed with the fragrance of incense and rain. Down a path and around the back, tucked out of sight, there is a special gallery.

In the gallery there are all sizes of vases, bowls, boxes, and plates. The variety of colors and patterns is dizzying. There are flowers, scenes of nature, and abstract designs. Looking closely, one can see that all the beautiful colors and shapes have not been painted on but are created by layer upon layer of different colored clays. This is a special technique in ceramics called neriage (NEH-REE-AH-GEH), which originated in China over one thousand years ago.

Ceramics, the oldest craft in Japan, is still the most popular. Matsui Kosei (MA-TSOO-EE KO-SAY) has taken neriage to

new heights. Using a variety of brilliantly colored clays, he carefully places one next to the other until it forms a big loaf. Then he slices it into slabs, which he shapes into bowls, vases, plates, or boxes. It sounds easy, but it is very difficult. In fact, Mr. Matsui keeps his own methods a secret, just like the Japanese craftsmen of old.

Mr. Matsui's ancestors have served as priests at the Gessho-ji temple for twenty-four generations, as Mr. Matsui does today. But he broke with tradition by choosing also to become a full-time potter. Luckily, on the grounds of the temple there was an unused pottery studio, which he reopened. Young Matsui felt the life of the potter calling him through a little teacup he discovered in his father's collection of antiques. It was just the right size for his hand, not perfectly shaped. As Mr. Matsui says, "The cup was formed poetically, purposely twisted."

Mr. Matsui went to school in Tokyo. He visited Tokyo National Museum almost every day to study antique ceramics and pottery. This was an important part of his training. Today, Mr. Matsui exhibits his work throughout the world and one of his creations is in the collection of the imperial family.

Left, *a glimpse into Mr. Matsui's showroom*

For Mr. Matsui, two things make an artist truly great: feeling and practice. "We are born equal. The most important thing is to nurture ourselves so we are aware of how we feel. When you see the ocean, rivers, stars, or desert, you are moved. . . . It's like electricity running down your spine. Your inner soul seems to connect with nature. Unfortunately the city life, with its endless stressful competition, creates a distance from nature. In the end, people forget to respect others and themselves in this world. To connect with people, culture, and tradition requires a sensitivity toward nature."

Mr. Matsui's apprentices begin their training by wedging clay every day for two years. Wedging is slamming and kneading clay on a table to force the air bubbles out. Mr. Matsui thinks that this hard work puts them in touch with the clay and, therefore, with nature. He feels deeply that the neriage technique can suggest the composition of the universe. The elements of many different colored clays refer to different people, cultures, and traditions. And the neriage vase, its shape and colors, suggests the surface of the earth.

MORE ABOUT NERIAGE

Matsui Kosei's neriage technique for making designs in clay is a secret that took him years of hard work to develop. Following tradition, he is passing his secrets on to his son. Here are the basic steps:

Hand–Building Method #1

1. Two or more different colors of clay are used. They are pressed together and shaped into a roll, like a jelly roll, or a loaf. With careful planning, many different shapes can be worked into a design.

2. The roll is sliced with a thin wire.

3. In this case, four slices are pressed and smoothed together to form one piece. The pieces are shaped into the sides and bottom of the work. The slices can also be pressed into a mold, such as a bowl.

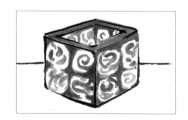

4. The edges are smoothed out.

5. The clay is then fired, or baked, in an oven called a kiln. After the first firing, an overglaze is applied, and the work is fired again. The glaze turns clear and brings out the color of the clays, adds a shiny finish, and makes them waterproof.

Hand–Building Method #2

1. As in method #1, and as always in the neriage technique, different-colored clays are used. Here, two (or more) colors of clay are rolled out into small slabs.

 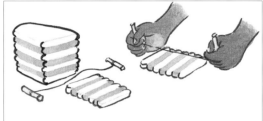

2. The colors are arranged in a pattern and stacked like a layer cake. Then the layers are sliced with a thin wire.

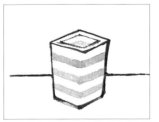

3. The slices are gently pressed together to form the sides and bottom of the work.

Steps 4 and 5 are the same as on page 46.

Using a Potter's Wheel

1. Two or more colors of clay are combined and shaped on a potter's wheel. The colors will mix together.

2. In this technique, the outside of the piece gets wet and sticky. But when the outer layer is scraped away, a free-form pattern is revealed underneath. The variations are endless! Then the piece is fired in a kiln, as on page 46.

For my grandparents—S.H.

For my parents, and for Nana Anakwa II
and all my students—A.O.

The text type is 13 1/2-point Nofret Light.

Published by Morrow Junior Books
a division of William Morrow and Company, Inc.
1350 Avenue of the Americas, New York, NY 10019

Book design by Claire B. Counihan

Printed in Singapore at Tien Wah Press.

2 3 4 5 6 7 8 9 10

Library of Congress Cataloging-in-Publication Data
Hamanaka, Sheila.
In search of the spirit: the living national treasures of Japan/by Sheila Hamanaka and Ayano
Ohmi; illustrations by Sheila Hamanaka; calligraphy by Ayano Ohmi.
p. cm.
Summary: Describes the creations of some of Japan's Living National Treasures, artists who are
involved in various Japanese arts, including yuzen dyeing, bamboo basket weaving,
Bunraku puppet making, sword making, Noh theater, and neriage ceramics.
ISBN 0-688-14607-4 (trade)—ISBN 0-688-14608-2 (library)
1. Arts, Japanese—Juvenile literature.   2. Artists—Japan—Biography—Juvenile literature.
[1. Arts, Japanese.   2. Artists.   3. Japan—Biography.]   I. Ohmi, Ayano.   II. Title.
NX584.A1H34 1999   700'.952—dc21   98-25051   CIP AC

PHOTO CREDITS
Jacket: sword by Fumiyasu Kaname; Iizuka Shokansai in his studio by Masao Ohmi; pp. 6 and
10, lower left, by kind permission of Moriguchi Kako; pp. 14, 16, left, and 17, right, from an
exhibition catalog of Mr. Iizuka's work, by kind permission of Mr. Iizuka and the Council of
Events, Ohta City, Japan; p. 17, left, by Masao Ohmi; pp. 28 and 29, top, by Fumiyasu Kaname;
pp. 32, 33 © 1995 by Tom Kishida; pp. 36, left, and 38 by kind permission of Kenichi Kasai,
Tessen-Kai. All other photographs were taken by Sheila Hamanaka.

INDEX